AF260960

Published by UTU Media® - © 2026 Bridget Irby
No part of this book may be reproduced or transmitted in any form or by any means, electronic or mechanical, including photocopying and recording, or by information storage or retrieval system, except as may be expressly permitted in writing by the publisher.
ISBN - 9781966130048
Unless indicated otherwise, all Scriptures marked KJV are taken from the KING JAMES VERSION (KJV): KING JAMES VERSION, public domain.
Printed in the United States of America

Dear Reader,
This Book Is Dedicated To You.

*Your journey may not always be easy but, it is worth it.*
*I pray you find the words inside helpful and healing.*

_Dear Friend,_

Have you ever felt it? That gentle whisper in your heart telling you that God has so much more for your life? That there's a deeper relationship with Him waiting just around the corner, if only you knew how to get there?

Maybe you're doing all the "right" things. You're reading your Bible (or at least trying to), showing up to church (most Sundays), and praying (even if sometimes it feels like your prayers are hitting the ceiling and bouncing right back). Yet somehow, it feels like you're stuck in spiritual quicksand – the more you struggle, the deeper you sink.

Here's the truth: Sometimes, the path to more of God isn't about doing more things right – **_it's about stopping the things that are holding you back_**.

This is exactly why I created the "You Are Not Called" series. These books aren't about adding more to your spiritual to-do list. Instead, they're about gaining freedom by doing less – freedom from anxiety that steals your peace, freedom from fear that holds you captive, freedom from anger that robs your joy, freedom from shame that keeps you hidden, and freedom from loneliness that makes you feel disconnected from God and others.

I'm not writing these books from some lofty spiritual mountaintop. I'm writing as someone who has crawled through the valleys of anxiety, fear, anger, shame, and loneliness – and discovered that God was there all along, waiting to show me a better way. As an ordained minister, yes, but more importantly, as a woman who has lived every word on these pages, I can tell you with absolute certainty: You are not called to live this way. You are not called to be anxious, afraid, angry, ashamed, or alone. These struggles are not your inheritance as a child of God.

Think of this series as your spiritual "stop it" list. Just like a gardener needs to pull out weeds before planting new seeds, we need to identify and remove the things that are choking our spiritual growth.

I've seen God's transformative power firsthand. Each book in this series represents a battle I've fought and won, not through my own strength, but through discovering what God says about who we are and what we're called to be.

This journey won't always be easy but I promise you this: if you're ready to let go of what's holding you back, if you're willing to challenge the lies you've believed, and if you're prepared to step into the freedom God has for you, your life will never be the same.  Because the truth is, sister, you were created for more than just surviving – you were created to thrive.

With faith, hope, and a whole lot of grace,

_Bridget_

_xoxo_

# Free Resources

Hey there, superstar!

I'm so proud of you for starting this journey and because I'm not about to send you out there empty-handed, I've got some awesome resources to help you on your journey.

Think of these as your toolkit. They're like the Swiss Army knife of emotional and spiritual growth - versatile, handy, and they might just save you in a pinch (though maybe don't try to use them to open a can or cut down a small tree).

To access the resources, simply create your free account at www.youarenotcalled.com.

Inside, you'll have to the above resources plus much more!

# A Not-So-Boring-But-Very-Important Disclaimer

## (Please Read This, Even If You Usually Skip These Things)

Before we dive into this adventure together, we need to have a little chat. You know, the kind that usually comes with a cup of coffee and a "Now, don't freak out, but..." opener. So, grab your beverage of choice (I won't judge if it's not coffee), and let's get real for a moment.

First things first: I am not a doctor, therapist, counselor, or any other type of licensed mental health professional. I know, shocking right? Despite my incredible ability to dispense wisdom and wit (if I do say so myself), my qualifications are more in the realm of "life experience" and "passionate Jesus follower" than "Ph.D. in Psychology."

This book, as awesome as it is (and trust me, it's pretty awesome), is not meant to replace the invaluable work of trained professionals. Think of it more as a heart-to-heart with a friend who's been there, done that, and got the t-shirt (and maybe a few therapy sessions) to prove it.

If you're dealing with severe anger issues, depression, anxiety, or any other mental health concerns, **please, please, PLEASE seek help from a qualified professional.** They have tools in their toolbox that go way beyond what I can offer here. *(Plus, they probably have comfier couches for you to sit on while you talk.)*

This book is meant to be a companion on your journey, not your only guide. It's like having a workout buddy – super helpful and motivating, but not a substitute for a trained physical therapist if you've got a serious injury.

So, if at any point while reading this book you think, "Wow, I could really use some professional help with this," then congratulations! You've just had an incredibly mature and self-aware moment. Seriously, give yourself a pat on the back, then go find yourself a therapist. Your future self will thank you.

Remember, seeking help is not a sign of weakness. It's a sign that you're brave enough to admit you don't have all the answers (welcome to the club, by the way) and smart enough to ask for guidance. That's the kind of wisdom that would make Solomon proud!

Now, with all that said, I truly believe that this book has the potential to be a powerful tool in your spiritual and emotional growth journey. Just think of it as one piece of your "becoming-the-best-version-of-yourself" puzzle, not the whole picture.

So, are we clear? This book = awesome friend and spiritual cheerleader. Trained professionals = necessary allies for serious stuff. You = amazing child of God who deserves all the help and support you can get.

Alright, now that we've got that out of the way, let's get back to the good stuff. You've got a life-changing journey ahead of you, and I, for one, can't wait to see where it takes you. Just remember, if the road gets too bumpy, don't be afraid to call in some professional reinforcements. After all, even Batman needed Alfred, right?

# Remember...

## There's no rush.

You and me, love, we've got our whole lives to figure this thing out.
Don't let rushing steal your joy.

## There's no wrong answer.

This is unique to you and you simply cannot get it wrong. Just be
honest with yourself and we can go from there.

## You are doing great.

High five sister! Just the fact that you are here, with God,
working on you says everything. Congratulations!

Week One

Shame's very first attack wasn't loud. It wasn't dramatic. It didn't roar onto the scene. It whispered. Immediately after Adam and Eve sinned, their first instinct wasn't to repent... it was to hide. They covered themselves, withdrew, and avoided God's presence. For the very first time in history, humankind felt the weight of an emotion God never intended us to carry: **shame**.

Shame didn't say, "You did something wrong." Shame said, "There is something wrong with you." Shame attacks identity, not behavior. Shame convinces you that you are unworthy, defective, broken, not enough, less-than, a disappointment, beyond repair. Shame wants you to believe that the worst thing about you is the truest thing about you. But over and over again in Scripture, God reveals the opposite. He calls the hiding out of darkness, the unworthy chosen, the broken beloved, the ashamed restored.

The voice of shame is always rooted in fear and separation. It says, "Hide. Don't let anyone see you. Don't let God near you." But the voice of God does the exact opposite — He draws near and calls us out. When God asks Adam, "Where are you?" in Genesis 3, He isn't asking because He lost track of Adam's location. He was after Adam's heart. He was naming the distance shame created. Shame always creates distance. God always closes it.

If you've been living under the belief that something is fundamentally wrong with you — that there is something about you God can't use, can't fix, can't redeem — hear this clearly: **there is nothing wrong with you that God cannot heal, restore, and repurpose for His glory**. Shame tells you to hide. God calls you to come near.

**READ GENESIS 3:7 (KJV)**

Spend time praying right now that God reveals to you what lie about your identity has been the hardest to shake and how shame has shaped how you see yourself. Journal your thoughts below.

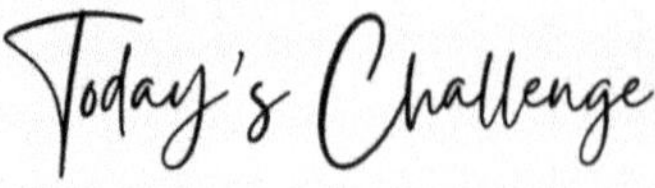


Today, take 5 quiet minutes with God.

Write down one sentence that captures your biggest shame-lie — the one

that plays loudest in your mind.


Then — cross it out.

Rewrite a biblical truth above it.


Example:

✗ "Something is wrong with me."

✓ "I am wonderfully made and deeply loved."


Place this truth somewhere visible today — on your phone, your mirror,

your journal. Speak it out loud every time shame tries to whisper.

# Day 2 – Shame Distorts How You See Yourself

Shame doesn't just whisper that something is wrong with you — it begins to shape how you see everything about yourself. It becomes a lens, a filter, a quiet narrator that sits in the back of your mind and comments on every thought, every mistake, every memory, every opportunity. Shame turns moments into identities, failures into labels, wounds into definitions, and experiences into verdicts. Without even realizing it, people begin to see themselves through the eyes of their past instead of the eyes of their Father.

You start to think things like: "I'm too messed up," "I'm too old," "I'm too late," "I'm not like other Christians," "I'm not enough," "I don't fit," "I don't belong," "I'm not worthy of being loved." Shame reduces you, shrinks who you believe you are, and convinces you to settle for a smaller story. But God never speaks to you through shame. When He speaks, He restores. When He corrects, He lifts. When He convicts, He cleanses — He never condemns.

Conviction says, "You're better than this. Let Me help you rise." Shame says, "This is who you are. You'll never change." Conviction calls you forward. Shame chains you backward. The truth is this: **you will never see yourself accurately until you see yourself through God's eyes**. And He calls you His daughter, His masterpiece, His creation, His delight, His beloved. There is nothing about you — not your past, struggles, mistakes, or journey — that disqualifies you from being fully loved by God. Shame may distort your reflection, but it cannot rewrite your identity. Only God can name you, and He has already called you "Mine."

## READ PSALM 139:14 (KJV)

Read the scripture, then spend time in prayer asking God to reveal to you what lies you have believed about your worth and what would change if you fully believed God's version of you.

Choose one thing today that reflects the truth of who God says you are — and practice it.

It could be:

- speaking one affirmation aloud

- initiating a kind conversation

- doing something bold you've avoided

- choosing rest instead of self-punishment

- journaling your strengths

- showing up fully instead of shrinking

Every time shame says "don't," do the opposite. These small steps begin to rewrite your internal narrative.

If shame could speak in a single sentence, it would say this: **"God is disappointed in you."** Shame convinces us that God is standing far away with His arms crossed, waiting for us to "get it together" before He loves us again. Shame tells us that every mistake lowers God's opinion of us. It makes God look harsh, distant, and unapproachable — like we have to earn our way back into His presence.

But that version of God is not the God of Scripture. Think of the prodigal son. Before the son apologized, before he cleaned up, before he became "worthy," the Father ran, embraced him, covered him, and restored him. That means the moment you turn toward God — even in your mess — He's already running toward you. Shame tells you God is withholding love. Grace tells you God is pouring it out. Shame says He's disappointed. Grace says He delights in you. Shame says you need to earn forgiveness. Grace says it's already paid for. Shame says you're too far gone. Grace says you're already home.

Every woman I've ever met who struggles with shame also struggles with approaching God confidently. Prayer feels scary. Worship feels undeserved. Reading the Bible feels intimidating. Even receiving love feels "too much." Shame hides you from God. Grace draws you to Him. But hear this clearly: **God does not view you through the lens of your past, your mistakes, or your shame. He views you through the finished work of Jesus.** When God looks at you, He sees clean, covered, chosen, redeemed, restored, loved, welcomed, daughter. He sees YOU — the real you. And He still moves toward you. God is not disappointed in you. He is not surprised by you. He is not hesitant with you. He is not withholding from you. He is the Father who runs.

# Bible Reading

**READ HEBREWS 4:16 (KJV)**

What is one thing you avoid bringing to God because of shame? Take some time to pray over this scripture with a heart that seeks God's will and clarity. Journal your thoughts and answers below.

Today, spend 5 minutes in honest, unfiltered prayer. Tell God exactly where you feel shame, fear, or hesitation. Don't clean it up. Don't make it neat. Just be real.

Then — picture the Father running toward you.

Arms open.

Face soft.

Heart moved.

Not because you "earned it," but because you turned toward Him.

Let yourself be seen — fully, deeply, safely.

Shame doesn't just attack your identity — it goes after your purpose. If shame can convince you there is something fundamentally wrong with you, the next lie it whispers is: **"God can't use you."** Shame tries to shrink your calling by shrinking you. It tells you that your past disqualifies you, your wounds limit you, and your mistakes cancel what God originally planned. Shame wants you to live small — quiet, hidden, safe, unavailable. It wants you to believe that God only uses the perfect, the polished, the put-together.

But look at Scripture. God chooses the most unlikely people every single time: Moses, who doubted himself; Gideon, who hid in fear; David, who failed publicly; Rahab, with a complicated past; Peter, who denied Jesus; Paul, with a history of violence. These were not perfect people. They were willing people.

Shame says, "Your past cancels your purpose." God says, "Your past is the platform for your purpose." Shame says, "Hide — you're not ready." God says, "Come — I'll prepare you." Shame says, "You can't lead, serve, speak, or build." God says, "My strength is made perfect in your weakness." Hear this clearly: **your purpose was written before your mistakes. Your calling isn't fragile. Your destiny is not canceled by your past.** Shame distorts how you see your purpose because it wants to keep you from becoming who God created you to be. But God is not done with you. He has not changed His mind about you. And He will not allow shame to steal what Jesus paid for. You are called, chosen, purposed, positioned. And nothing — not even shame — can undo that.

## READ ROMANS 11:29 (KJV)

What do you think today's reading means in the context of your life? What calling or dream have you avoided because you feel unqualified? Journal your thoughts below after reading and spending time in prayer.

# Today's Challenge

Today, take one small step toward your God-given purpose.

It doesn't need to be big. It just needs to be bold.

- Send the message.

- Write the idea down.

- Brainstorm the dream.

- Look up the resource.

- Pray the dangerous prayer.

- Say "yes" to the thing you've been avoiding.

Do something that contradicts shame and aligns with calling.

Purpose grows with movement.

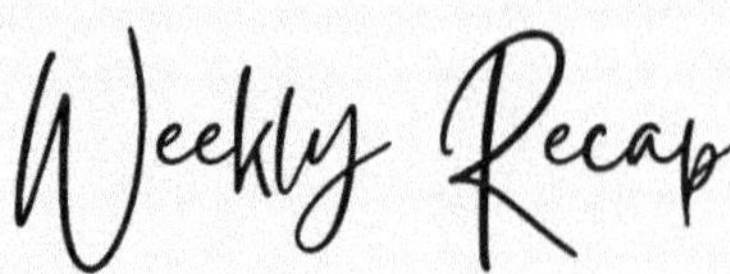



This week, you uncovered the foundations of shame — where it comes from, how it distorts your identity, how it twists your view of God, and how it tries to sabotage your purpose. You learned that shame isn't conviction, and it isn't correction. Shame is spiritual attack disguised as self-judgment.

You confronted the first lie shame ever told: **"Something is wrong with me."** You saw how shame warps your reflection and speaks over your identity, telling you who you're not instead of reminding you who you are. You learned that God sees you through the lens of grace — not failure — and that He draws near even when you withdraw.

You discovered that shame doesn't just affect how you see yourself; it tries to make you believe that God sees you differently too. But Scripture makes it clear: He runs toward you, not away from you. And finally, you learned the truth shame fears most: **your purpose is not fragile, your calling is not revocable, your destiny is not canceled**, your past does not intimidate God, your mistakes do not disqualify you, your shame does not define you.

This week was about exposing lies. The next weeks will be about uprooting them — and replacing them with truth, freedom, confidence, and restoration. Take a breath. Take a moment. Let your heart settle into this truth: **shame is not your inheritance. Freedom is.**

Father,
Thank you for revealing the truth about shame.

Thank You for showing me that shame isn't from You, and it isn't who I am.

Wash over every part of me that has been shaped by shame — my identity, my thoughts, my decisions, and my purpose.

Help me see myself the way You see me.

Help me trust that You are not disappointed in me.

Break every lie that shame has spoken, and fill me with Your confidence and peace. I am Yours.

In Jesus' name,
Amen.

Week Two

# Day 1: Shame Rooted In Sin Or Mistakes

One of the most common roots of shame is this: **"I did something wrong... so I am wrong."** Shame takes a moment — a decision, a season, a stumble — and turns it into an identity. It attaches your worst choices to your name and says, "This is who you are now." But God does not do that. Scripture makes a clear distinction between **guilt**, **repentance**, and **shame**. Guilt says, "I made a wrong choice." Repentance says, "I'm turning back toward God." Shame says, "God doesn't want me anymore." Only one of these is a lie — and it's shame. God never defines you by your regrets. He never ties your identity to your failures. When Jesus died on the cross, He carried every sin you could ever confess — and every ounce of shame attached to it.

Shame keeps reminding you of your past. Grace keeps reminding you it's forgiven. Shame drags you into who you used to be. Grace calls you into who you're becoming. If your deepest shame comes from decisions you made — mistakes, relationships, choices you wish you could undo — hear this clearly: **God knew every moment of your story when He called you.** And He called you anyway. You cannot shock Him. You cannot disappoint Him into withdrawing His love. You cannot out-sin the reach of His grace.

Your past may explain your journey, but it does not determine your destiny. Your identity is defined by God's grace, not your mistakes. Forgiveness is final — shame is optional. God wants you to live in the freedom that comes from knowing your failures do not disqualify you from His love. He invites you to leave shame behind and step fully into the truth of who you are in Him.

READ, REFLECT, & PRAY ON
ROMANS 8:1 (KJV)

**Journal Prompt:**

What would happen if you stopped

calling yourself by your past?

# Today's Challenge

Write a letter (just for yourself) to the version of you who made that mistake.

Speak to her with compassion; tell her what you know now; tell her what God says

about her; tell her she is forgiven. Tell her she can come home.

Then pray over that letter.

Let God rewrite your memory of that season.

Some shame doesn't start with what you did. It starts with what you were taught to believe about yourself. Childhood shame is powerful because it often begins before you have the language to understand it. Maybe you grew up in a home that was chaotic, critical, unpredictable, emotionally absent, or spiritually heavy-handed. Maybe you were compared, dismissed, overlooked, or told you were "too much" or "not enough." Children internalize these messages. Instead of thinking, "My environment is unhealthy," they think, "I must be the problem." That belief becomes a quiet script that follows you into adulthood.

Shame rooted in childhood sounds like: "I'm hard to love," "I have to earn affection," "If I don't perform, I'll be rejected," "My needs are a burden," "If I don't stay strong, everything falls apart." But what your family couldn't give you does not determine your worth. What people spoke over you is not what God speaks over you. God does not parent you the way people did. He does not love conditionally or withdraw affection when you struggle. He is steady where others were unpredictable, gentle where others were harsh, present where others were absent.

You are not the product of your upbringing. You are the product of God's intentional design. He sees you fully, loves you completely, and is writing a story that shame cannot dictate. The beliefs you internalized as a child can be replaced by His truth. God re-parents you with affirmation, compassion, and belonging, giving you what was never fully received before.

# Bible Reading



**Journal Prompt:**

What do you wish someone had told you

growing up?

Today, speak one healing truth to your younger self, picture her and see her clearly. Then give her what she never received — affirmation, compassion, belonging, safety. Let God's voice be the one that surrounds her.

# Day 3 – Shame Rooted in Relationships

Some of the deepest shame doesn't come from what you did — it comes from what someone else chose. When someone walks away, rejects you, cheats, betrays your trust, abandons you, or chooses someone else over you, shame whispers: "If you were enough, they wouldn't have left," "If you were lovable, they wouldn't have betrayed you," "If you mattered, they would've stayed." But someone else's choices do not determine your worth. Rejection is not a reflection of your value. Betrayal is not proof that you're unlovable. Divorce is not an indictment of your identity. Someone walking away does not mean you weren't worth staying for.

Shame attaches itself to heartbreak because it looks for vulnerability. When you're hurting, shame tries to convince you the pain is your fault — even when it isn't. But hear this clearly: you cannot control someone else's decisions, and their choices cannot change your God-given worth. God does not look at you through the lens of what someone did to you. He looks at you through the lens of what Jesus did for you. He has never withdrawn His love. If someone left — God did not. If someone rejected you — God chose you. If someone betrayed you — God stands for you.

Your story didn't end when they walked away. God is writing a chapter that shame has no right to interrupt. He remains faithful, constant, and present. Your worth is anchored in His love, not other people's actions. Every rejection is an opportunity to see God's faithfulness more clearly and lean fully on Him.

# Bible Reading

## READ, REFLECT, & PRAY ON
## PSALM 34:18 (KJV)

**Journal Prompt:**

What relationship hurt left a shame

imprint on your heart?

Write this sentence somewhere you can see it today:

"Their choices do not define me — God does."

Every time your mind drifts back to rejection or abandonment, come back to this truth. Let it anchor you. Let it silence shame.

This is one of the heaviest and most complicated forms of shame — the shame that comes from trauma or abuse. It attaches itself to something you did not choose, did not want, and did not deserve. Trauma convinces you that you were the problem. Abuse whispers lies like: "I should've known better," "I should've stopped it," "I should've spoken up," "I did something to cause it," "I'm damaged now," "I'm unworthy because of what happened to me." But none of these things are true. Trauma and abuse create wounds, but they do not define identity. What happened to you is not who you are.

God does not agree with the lies trauma speaks. He does not blame you. He does not shame you. He does not expect you to "get over it." He moves with compassion, authority, and healing. Jesus repeatedly moved toward the broken, the shamed, the outcast, and the wounded. He dignified women nobody else honored, restored those society rejected, and lifted the crushed by shame. Your trauma is not hidden from God, but neither is His healing hidden from you.

God restores dignity, identity, innocence, and the parts of your heart the enemy tried to destroy. You are not "ruined." You are not "less than." You are not "too much." You are not "too broken." You are His daughter — whole, loved, chosen, and being healed layer by layer. This week, God calls you to see yourself through His eyes, not the lies trauma speaks, and to walk into His restoration one step at a time.

READ, REFLECT, & PRAY ON
PSALM 147:3 (KJV)

**Journal Prompt:**

What lie have you believed about yourself

because of what happened?

Today, let yourself acknowledge this truth:
What happened to me is not who I am.

Say it out loud.
Say it slowly.
Say it with compassion for your own story.

Then invite God to begin healing one layer, one memory, one wound at a time.

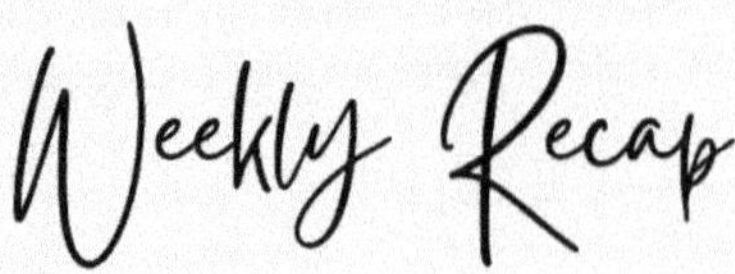

# Weekly Recap

This week, you explored where shame originates — not from who you are, but from what you've lived through. You learned that shame from sin is healed by forgiveness, shame from childhood is healed by truth, shame from relationships is healed by God's faithfulness, and shame from trauma is healed by God's compassion. You saw that shame does not appear at random. It has roots, stories, and moments where it entered — sometimes loudly, sometimes quietly.

You recognized something important: you can't heal what you won't name. This week wasn't about reliving pain; it was about revealing patterns. It was about taking shame out of the shadows and putting truth in its place. You began to separate your identity from your experiences. You began to see yourself apart from your past. You began to understand that shame isn't a character trait — it's a wound God intends to heal.

Your courage is holy. Your honesty is powerful. Your healing has already begun. Next week, you'll expose the lies shame has been speaking over your life — and replace every one of them with God's truth. This is your invitation to live fully in the freedom God provides, to step into the truth of who He created you to be, and to leave shame where it belongs — in the past.

# Weekly Prayer

Dear Father,

Thank you for revealing the roots of shame in my life.

Thank you for showing me that shame is not my identity, and it is not my future.

Heal every wound at the root.

Break every lie that grew from painful experiences.

Restore my heart with truth, gentleness, and clarity.

I trust You with every part of my story — even the pieces that hurt.

Continue healing me as I move into next week.

In Jesus' name,
Amen.

Week Three

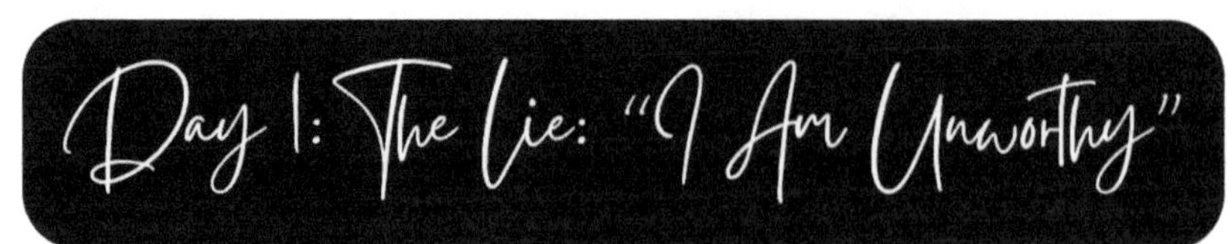


Shame loves to attack the very core of who you are. If shame had a favorite sentence, it would be: "You aren't worthy of love, blessings, or belonging." This lie usually begins subtly — a disappointment here, a rejection there, a moment where you feel unseen or overlooked. Slowly, shame whispers that maybe you just aren't worth choosing. But that is NOT God's voice. God calls you worthy not because of what you've done — but because of who He is. You are worthy because God created you with intention, Jesus redeemed you with purpose, and the Holy Spirit dwells within you with power. Your worth is anchored in heaven, not in human perception.

Unworthiness says, "I don't deserve good things." God says, "You were designed for good things" (Ephesians 2:10). Unworthiness says, "I'm too broken to be loved." God says, "You are loved with an everlasting love" (Jeremiah 31:3). Unworthiness says, "Something about me is fundamentally wrong." God says, "You are fearfully and wonderfully made" (Psalm 139:14). Your worth is not something you earn — it's something you inherit. If shame has convinced you to perform, impress, or prove yourself, breathe this in: you were worthy before anyone else had an opinion, before a single mistake, and because God chose you first.

This lie dies the moment you accept that your worth is not on trial. Your identity is not conditional or negotiable. Every choice, success, or failure cannot change the truth God has spoken over you. You are deeply loved, intentionally made, and fully chosen. You don't have to earn it, and no one can take it away.

**Journal Prompt:**

What would change if you fully believed

God chose you?

# Today's Challenge

Speak this out loud today:

"I am worthy because God says I am — not because I feel like it."

Bonus: Write down three verses about your worth and place them where you'll see

them.

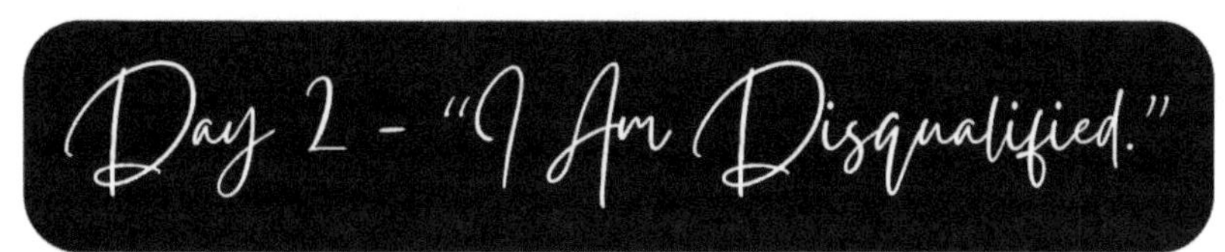


Shame whispers that your past removes you from God's plans. It says, "You missed your chance," "You messed up too badly," "Someone like you can't be used by God." But this is one of shame's biggest lies. God's story is full of people who "should have been" disqualified. Moses murdered a man. David committed adultery and orchestrated a death. Peter denied Jesus publicly. Paul violently persecuted the church. And God used every single one of them powerfully. Your calling is based on God's power, not your perfection.

Shame says, "You're done." God says, "I'm not finished" (Philippians 1:6). Shame says, "Your history is too messy." God says, "My grace is sufficient, even in your weakness" (2 Corinthians 12:9). Shame says, "You've disqualified yourself." God says, "My call is irrevocable" (Romans 11:29). You cannot disqualify what God qualified. Your past may explain you, shape you, or even break parts of you, but it cannot cancel what God ordained. You are not disqualified — you are being prepared.

God's grace is bigger than every mistake, every misstep, and every regret. Your worthiness and purpose are not on probation. You are invited to step into God's plan today, even if it feels too late or too messy. Movement, even small, is the antidote to shame.

READ, REFLECT, & PRAY ON
ROMANS 11:29 (KJV)

**Journal Prompt:**

What calling or dream have you avoided

because you feel disqualified?

Name one area where shame has convinced you to hold back.

Today, take one small step toward it — even if it's tiny.

Movement is the enemy of shame.

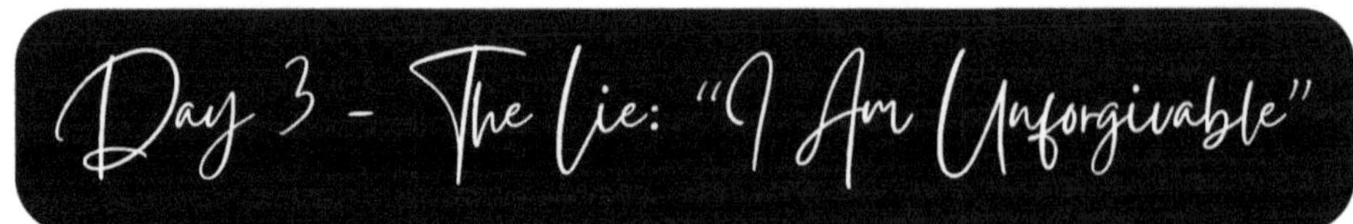


This is one of shame's cruelest lies — the belief that you have done something God cannot forgive. Shame points to memories that still sting, choices you wish you could erase, seasons you wish you could rewrite, and it whispers, "God forgives others, but not that."

But here is the truth: there is no category of sin stronger than the blood of Jesus. If Jesus' sacrifice isn't enough for your worst moment, then it isn't enough for anyone. When Jesus said, "It is finished," He meant it. Forgiveness is not partial, conditional, or probationary. It does not expire. It is full, complete, and final.

Unforgivable is a human word, not a heavenly one. The enemy wants you to believe this lie because if he can keep you enslaved to shame, he can keep you from stepping into freedom. But God already declared you forgiven. He already removed your sin "as far as the east is from the west." He already said He will "remember it no more." He already washed it clean. The question becomes: if God has forgiven you, why should shame still have a say?

Your past mistakes cannot cancel God's mercy. You can step forward in freedom, knowing every wrong is covered by grace.

You can live today in the assurance that His forgiveness is complete and eternal.

# Bible Reading

**READ, REFLECT, & PRAY ON**
**1 JOHN 1:9 (KJV)**

**Journal Prompt:**

Where do you struggle to receive grace?

## Today's Challenge

Today, practice receiving grace.

Say, out loud:

"I am forgiven — fully, completely, and forever."

Even if it feels uncomfortable, keep saying it.

Your heart will catch up to your confession.

This lie keeps more Christians in shame than almost anything else. It sounds spiritual, but it is not. Shame twists God into someone He isn't — distant, frustrated, fed up, or tired of you. It makes you believe God is shaking His head saying, "Really? Again?" But this is NOT who God is. If God were easily disappointed, the prodigal son never would've been embraced. Peter never would've been restored. David never would've been crowned. Paul never would've been appointed. God's posture toward His children is compassion — not condemnation.

Disappointment focuses on flaws. God focuses on identity. Disappointment withdraws affection. God draws closer. Disappointment says, "Do better." God says, "Come to Me." Shame wants you to think God is looking at you through the lens of your failures. But God sees you through the lens of Jesus' finished work. He is not disgusted with you. He is not tired of you. He is not angry with you. He delights in you, even as you heal, grow, and stumble forward.

Your Father does not measure you by your progress or perfection. He moves toward you with holy love, grace, and delight. You are never too much, too messy, or too flawed to receive His embrace. Your identity is secure in Him, and His devotion is steadfast.

# Bible Reading

## READ, REFLECT, & PRAY ON
## PSALM 145:8 (KJV)

**Journal Prompt:**

When did you first feel like God was

disappointed in you?

Tell God the truth about where you feel He's disappointed.

Say it out loud or write it down.

Then ask Him:

"Lord, how do You actually see me?"

Listen.

He will answer.

This week, you exposed the lies shame uses to keep women hidden — unworthiness, disqualification, unforgiveness, and God's supposed disappointment. Each lie had a root, a story, and a moment where it wounded your identity. But each had a truth that dismantled it. You recognized that you are worthy because God says you are, called because God decided it, forgiven because Jesus finished it, and loved because God delights in you.

Shame tries to speak loudly — but truth speaks with authority. This week wasn't about learning new information; it was about breaking spiritual agreements you may not have realized you made. Where shame says, "Hide," truth says, "Heal." Where shame says, "Stay small," truth says, "Stand up." Where shame says, "God is disappointed," truth says, "He is running toward you."

This week marked the beginning of a new internal narrative — one rooted in Scripture, love, identity, and grace. Your freedom begins by believing the truths God has spoken, rejecting lies that steal your peace, and stepping fully into the life He designed for you.

Dear Lord,

Break the lie that You are disappointed in me.

Show me Your compassion.

Teach me to see Your heart clearly.

Draw me close and rewrite every distorted belief I hold about You.

In Jesus' name,
Amen.

Week Four

# Day 1: Letting God Heal What You Hide

Shame thrives in secrecy. It grows in the shadows of the things you avoid, the memories you never talk about, and the wounds you've learned to "manage" rather than heal. Shame convinces you that hiding is safer — that bringing your pain into God's presence is too risky. But hiding is not protection. Hiding is isolation. And isolation is where shame strengthens its grip. Adam and Eve hid after shame first entered the world, and we have been hiding in different ways ever since. But God's response has always been the same: He comes looking for us, not to punish, not to expose, but to heal.

When God asked Adam, "Where are you?" He wasn't confused about Adam's location — He was inviting Adam out of hiding so He could restore him. God still asks you the same question today: "Where are you? Where are you hiding? Where are you hurting? Where are you pretending to be fine?" Healing begins when hiding ends. God cannot heal the version of you that you pretend to be. He heals the real you — the honest you — the unfiltered you — the version that says, "Lord, this still hurts."

You don't have to bring Him the polished parts, the perfect prayer, or a cleaned-up story. You just bring your heart. And God brings the healing. He meets your shame where it lives and transforms it with His presence. What you've kept secret, what you've feared to admit, what you thought was too broken for God — He wants to restore it, gently, intentionally, fully.

Healing begins with honesty. Acknowledge the pain, bring it to God, and trust His loving hands to work. The hidden corners of your heart are not off-limits. They are exactly where His restoration begins. Invite Him in. Let Him shine His light. Let Him restore what shame tried to bury. Layer by layer, the real you is being made whole again.

**READ PSALM 34:18 (KJV)**

**Journal Prompt:**

What part of your story do you still hide from
God or others?

# Today's Challenge

Today, write one sentence of brutal honesty to God about the wound you've been

hiding.

Don't filter it.

Don't clean it up.

Don't adjust it to sound "Christian."

Just be real.

This is the doorway to healing.

Your past may explain you, but it does not own you. Shame tries to attach your identity to past seasons, decisions, relationships, or failures. It whispers that where you've been is the ultimate definition of who you are. But that is a lie. You are not the girl who made that mistake. You are not the woman who stayed too long. You are not the version of yourself who didn't know better. You are not the sum of your regrets, your lowest moment, or your hardest season. You are who God says you are — even on the days you don't feel like it

.

Releasing shame from your past doesn't mean pretending it never happened or that it didn't matter. It means reclaiming authority over the story shame tried to steal. Your past is a place of reference, not residence. Paul said, "Forgetting what is behind and pressing toward what is ahead..." He wasn't saying he lost his memory; he was saying, "I refuse to let my past define my present or dictate my future." You can't change what happened, but God can change what it means.

God steps into the moments you're most ashamed of and rewrites them with grace, purpose, and restoration. Shame ties you to who you used to be. Healing ties you to who God is making you. Your story is not over. Every regret, mistake, and failure is an opportunity for God to display His redemption.

Take authority today. Speak truth over the parts of your past that still carry shame. Invite God to redeem what once felt too heavy to bear. Let His grace transform the meaning of your memories, turning brokenness into a testimony, and shame into freedom.

# Bible Reading

## READ 2 CORINTHIANS 5:17
## (KJV)

**Journal Prompt:**

What part of your past still carries shame?

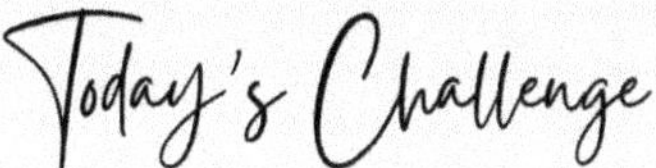


Choose one moment from your past that carries shame.

Speak this truth over it:

"This moment does not define me — God does."

Then pray for God to rewrite the meaning of that memory.

# Day 3 – Healing Shame Around Sex And Purity

This is one of shame's deepest and most common battlegrounds — sexuality, purity, and the body. For many women, shame whispers loudest here. Some feel shame around past sexual decisions, experiences forced upon them, or how their body looks, feels, or has changed. Others were raised with heavy-handed purity culture that taught fear instead of freedom. But hear this clearly: God does not shame you for this part of your story. He heals it. Jesus treated women with sexual wounds differently than society did. He didn't shame, expose, or condemn them. He lifted, defended, restored, and dignified them. Culture brings shame; God brings restoration.

Your body is not a source of shame — it is a temple. Your past doesn't stain you — Jesus cleanses you. Your sexuality is not dirty — it is sacred. Your story is not "too much" — it is redeemable. Whether your shame comes from choices you regret or experiences you never wanted, God responds with love, dignity, and restoration.

You are invited to step into that restoration today. Speak God's truth over your body, your sexuality, and your past. Let His voice rewrite the lies shame has told you. Embrace the freedom He offers. Let your identity be anchored in the Creator who made you, redeemed you, and calls you holy.

Step forward with courage. Accept God's healing over your sexuality and your body. Invite Him to cleanse, restore, and renew every part of your story. Layer by layer, allow the truth of His love to replace shame with dignity, grace, and wholeness.

READ JOHN 8:11 (KJV)

**Journal Prompt:**

Where has shame touched your sexuality or your body?

<h1 style="text-align:center;">Today's Challenge</h1>

Write a declaration today:

"My body is not a source of shame — it is a temple.

My past is not a stain — it is forgiven.

My story is not ruined — it is redeemed."

Speak it over yourself all day.

# Day 4 – Healing The Shame Of Failure

Failure is one of the enemy's favorite tools to create shame — not because failure is final, but because it feels personal. Failure tells you, "You're not capable," "You're not smart enough," "You'll mess it up again." But failure is not identity. Failure is an event. It is a moment, not a label. Scripture shows that God often uses failure as the soil for growth, wisdom, and calling. Peter failed dramatically, and Jesus built His church through him. David failed repeatedly, and God called him a man after His heart. Paul failed violently, and God transformed him into a pillar of the church. Failure does not disqualify you. Shame does.

Failure says, "Learn." Shame says, "Hide." Failure says, "Grow." Shame says, "Give up." Failure says, "Try again." Shame says, "Don't bother." Today, God wants to break the agreement between failure and shame in your life. You are not your mistakes, inconsistencies, or unfinished stories. You are growing, learning, and becoming.

Every fall is proof that God is shaping you. Every getting up is evidence that shame didn't win. You are on a path of transformation, and each step matters. Failure is the soil. God's grace is the water. Your obedience is the seed. And the harvest? Redemption, purpose, and proof that shame no longer defines you.

Trust Him with your next step. Step forward in courage, even if it's small. Allow failure to teach, not label. Allow God to redeem every misstep. And let His love break the power shame has held over your heart for far too long.

# *Bible Reading*

## READ PROVERBS 24:16 (KJV)

**Journal Prompt:**
Where has failure created shame in your life, and
what did it teach you?

## Today's Challenge

Identify one area where failure made you retreat.

Do one thing today that moves you forward again — however small.

Movement breaks shame.

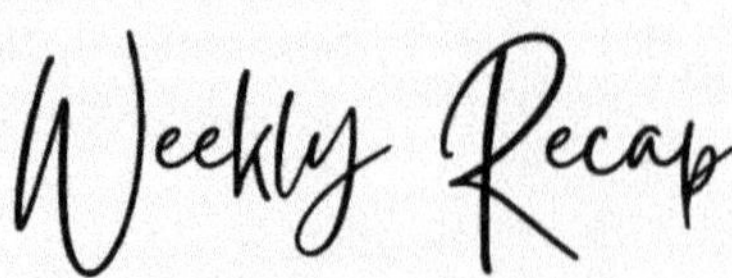

# Weekly Recap

This week, you stepped courageously into the deep places where shame has lived — the hidden parts of your past, your body, your sexuality, and your failures. These are the areas shame tries hardest to bury because God intends to heal them most profoundly. You explored what it looks like to bring hidden wounds into the light, to release shame from your past, and to invite God's restoration over every part of your story.

You discovered that hiding only delays healing. God is gentle with raw places. Your past does not define you. Your body is not a source of shame. Failure is not your identity. And in all these areas, God is restoring you — layer by layer, memory by memory, wound by wound.

This week wasn't about re-opening pain. It was about lifting shame off of it so healing could reach deep inside. You began to let God move in the places you have carried alone, places you may have believed were too broken to touch. You invited His love to rewrite your story and redefine your identity.

Healing is happening. Slowly. Gently. Deeply. Holistically. Next week, you will step into one of the most important parts of your transformation: discovering who you truly are — not according to shame, but according to God.

# Weekly Prayer

Dear Father,

thank You for meeting me in the places shame once ruled.

Thank You for healing the wounds I've carried and for restoring the parts of me I long believed were broken.

Continue to heal me layer by layer. Give me strength to release shame fully and confidently step into truth.

Let Your love restore every part of my identity.

In Jesus' name,
Amen.

Week Five

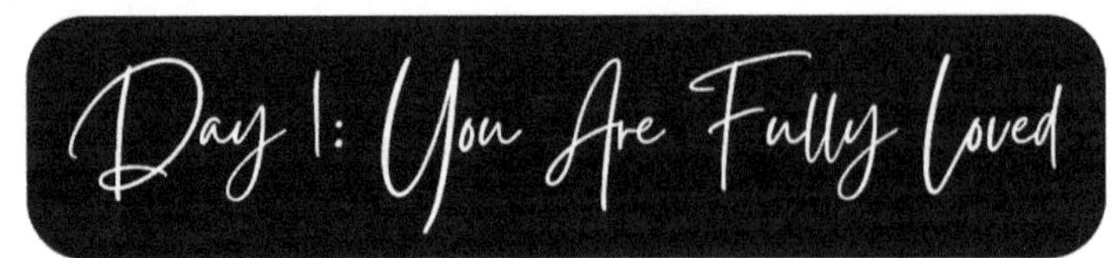


Shame says, "You're loved... but barely." "You're loved... but conditionally." "You're loved... but not like others." It whispers that God's love is fragile, dependent on your performance, or rationed. But that is a lie.

God's love is not cautious. It is not limited. It is not conditional. It is lavished on you — poured out abundantly, without hesitation or measure. This love is constant, unchanging, and eternal. The first truth God restores when shame attacks your identity is this: you are fully loved. Not partially, not sometimes, not when you meet the standard — fully, completely, and unconditionally.

Before you performed, before you improved, before you tried harder, before you healed, before you broke — He loved you. Nothing you have done or will ever do can outweigh that love. Shame tells you love should be earned; God says it is inherited. Shame says you must prove your worth; God says you were worthy before your first breath. This is not abstract theology; it is the foundation of your identity.

You will never live freely, confidently, or boldly until you embrace this truth: you are loved as you are. Not the future you, not the improved you, not the spiritual you — today's you. God's love is the most stable anchor for your soul. Accept it. Rest in it. Let it drown out the lies of shame and speak directly to your heart.

# Bible Reading

READ JEREMIAH 31:3 (KJV)

**Journal Prompt:**

What conditions have you placed on being
loved?

Today's Challenge

Today, sit still for 3 minutes.

No prayer requests.

No apologies.

No fixing.

Just sit in God's love.

Let it wash over you.

Let it speak louder than shame.

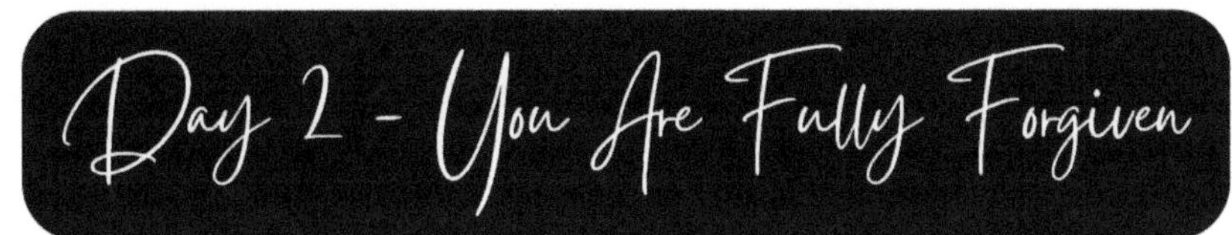


Shame thrives where forgiveness is misunderstood. It wants you to believe that some sins are too big, too obvious, too shameful to be fully forgiven. You may feel like your mistakes are exceptions, moments God can forgive everyone else for — but not you.

But Scripture is clear: forgiveness is full, final, and finished. When Jesus said, "It is finished," He meant no lingering guilt, no half-hearted cleansing, no spiritual probation. Your forgiveness is complete. You are not "mostly forgiven" or "forgiven but…" You are fully forgiven. And shame's power rests entirely on your agreement with its lies.

When you agree with God instead of shame, the lie loses its grip. You cannot change the past, but Jesus already changed your record. Every sin, every misstep, every regret is separated from you "as far as the east is from the west." There is no overlap. God's forgiveness is not fragile; it is eternal, complete, and active in your life today.

You are free to walk in the reality of this forgiveness. You are no longer bound by guilt or condemnation. You are clean. You are restored. The moment you choose to believe it, shame loses authority, and your heart can finally rest in the grace God has already poured over you.

# Bible Reading



**Journal Prompt:**

What forgiven sin do you still feel ashamed of?

Write this on a note:

"I am fully forgiven — and I choose to agree with God today."

Every time shame tries to revisit the past, speak it aloud.

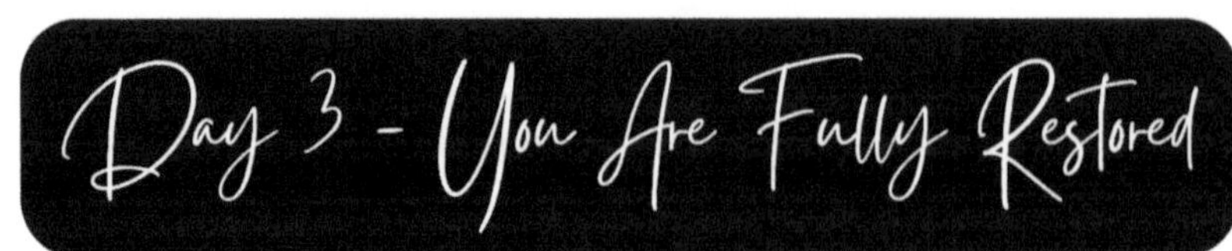


Shame says the damage is permanent. It says you'll never be whole again. It tells you your confidence, innocence, trust, joy, and hope are gone forever. But God does not do partial restoration — He restores fully.

Restoration doesn't ignore the past. It doesn't pretend nothing happened. It rebuilds, repairs, redeems, and renews everything shame has tried to destroy. You are not a broken woman limping through life; you are evidence of God's redemptive power. Your story is not defined by scars — it is defined by the God who restores them.

You may feel missing pieces of yourself — confidence, trust, identity, or joy — but God restores each one. He does not settle for patching old wounds; He forms a stronger, wiser, deeper version of you. Restoration is about becoming who God always intended you to be, not returning to a previous version of yourself.

Shame may try to keep you looking at what's lost, but God calls your eyes to what's renewed. He restores what was stolen, lost, or broken. He renews your purpose, heals your heart, and equips you for the future. You are not incomplete — you are becoming whole in Him.

**READ JOEL 2:25 (KJV)**

**Journal Prompt:**

What part of you feels the most "broken"?

Today's Challenge

Write a declaration:

"God restores me — fully, deeply, beautifully."

Say it throughout the day.

Let your spirit begin to believe it.

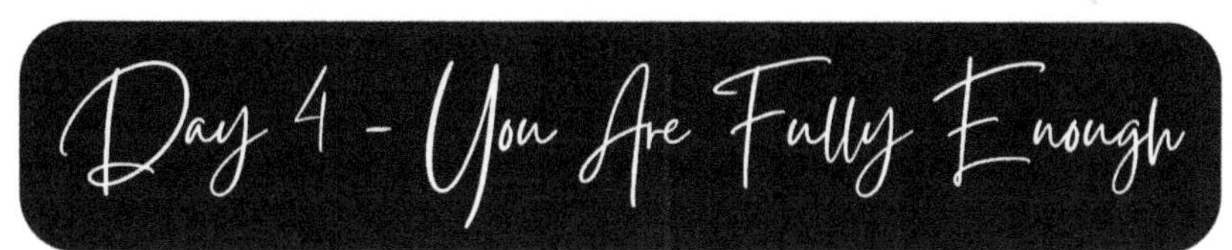


Shame whispers that you are not enough: not spiritual enough, not disciplined enough, not healed enough, not worthy enough. It tries to keep you exhausted, insecure, and performing constantly. But God's truth cancels every one of these lies.

You were never called to "be enough" — you were called to belong to Him. When He is enough, you are enough. You don't have to hold it all together; He holds you. You don't have to be perfect; He is perfect on your behalf. Grace fills every gap that shame insists you must cover.

Your worth does not depend on performance, appearance, intelligence, or spirituality. You are enough because God placed His Spirit inside you. You are chosen, worthy, loved, whole, and His. His voice always outranks shame. When you believe this truth, your freedom, confidence, and peace multiply.

Rest in this reality today. Stop carrying unnecessary expectations. Stop trying to earn a status that you already have. Let God's sufficiency cover every gap. You are fully enough because He is.

# *Bible Reading*

## READ 2 CORINTHIANS 12:9
## (KJV)

### Journal Prompt:

Where do you feel "not enough"?

# Today's Challenge

Today, stop one unnecessary expectation you've placed on

yourself.

Release it.

Let grace fill the gap.

Let yourself rest — without guilt.

# Weekly Recap

This week, you stepped into the truth of your identity — the identity shame tried to bury.

You learned that you are:
◆ Fully loved
◆ Fully forgiven
◆ Fully restored
◆ Fully enough

These truths are not dependent on your performance. They are rooted in God's character, not your perfection. You traded shame for identity, lies for truth, fear for confidence, condemnation for restoration, and weakness for grace.

You were never meant to live under the weight of shame's labels. Each day this week, God reminded you who you truly are — His beloved daughter. He spoke over you that your worth is not earned, your failures do not define you, your past does not disqualify you, and your scars are not a measure of inadequacy.

Shame may have tried to tell you that you were "barely enough," "too broken," or "unworthy of love." But God whispered the opposite: you are fully loved, fully forgiven, fully restored, and fully enough.

This week was about more than just learning truths; it was about letting them sink deep into your heart and reshape your thinking, your feelings, and your identity. You practiced hearing God's voice over shame, agreeing with His promises, and rejecting lies that tried to hold you back.

As you step into next week, carry this truth with you: your identity is secure in Christ. Nothing can take it away, and nothing can override it. Let the freedom, confidence, and assurance you discovered this week guide how you live, think, love, and trust God.

Dear Father,

Thank You for restoring my identity.

Thank You for showing me who I truly am in You — loved, forgiven, restored, and enough.

Rebuild my confidence in Your truth and silence every lie shame has spoken.

Let this identity take root in my heart and shape how I live, think, love, and trust You.

In Jesus' name,
Amen.

Week Six

Shame doesn't disappear all at once. Even after God heals, restores, and rewrites the truth, shame will still try to revisit—not because it owns you, but because it's familiar. It lingers in the corners of your mind, waiting for moments of weakness, insecurity, or self-doubt. Freedom is not a feeling you wait for. Freedom is a choice you practice, moment by moment, thought by thought.

Every time a thought rises that says, "You're not enough," "Remember what you did," "You should be ashamed," or "You don't deserve love," you get to respond with truth. Freedom is a muscle. The more you use it, the stronger it becomes. That's why Scripture calls us to "take every thought captive"—not just evil or destructive thoughts, but every shame-laced, lying, or accusatory thought.

Walking in freedom means recognizing the lie quickly, rejecting it immediately, and replacing it with truth intentionally. It's about refusing to replay old tapes of guilt or failure. Shame will always whisper. Freedom whispers back: "Not today. Not anymore. Not me." Choosing freedom means you're not returning to old patterns or slipping backwards. You are actively practicing your new identity, and practice creates permanence.

Every small choice adds up. Each moment you resist shame strengthens your confidence and rewires your heart. Over time, these repeated acts of courage form a pattern: your identity in Christ becomes louder than the lies, your voice becomes steadier than shame's whispers, and your soul begins to feel lighter, freer, and more secure. God has already set you free; your daily choice is to live like it.

Freedom is not passive. It requires awareness, intention, and courage. But with every thought you capture, every lie you reject, and every truth you claim, freedom becomes your habit, your mindset, and ultimately, your lifestyle.

# Bible Reading

## READ GALATIANS 5:1 (KJV)

**Journal Prompt:**

What shame-based thought returns most often?

Today, write down your most repeated shame-lie.

Then write the Scriptural truth that defeats it.

Read the truth 3 times today.

Shame will always try to return, which is why freedom requires boundaries. Just as you set boundaries with unhealthy people, you also set boundaries with unhealthy thoughts. Boundaries with shame sound like: "You don't speak for me," "You don't get access to my identity," "You don't get to define my worth," "You don't get to rewrite my past," and "You don't get to dictate my future."

Shame is bold. It will show up uninvited, attempt to sit in the seat of your mind, and act like it belongs there. But freedom says, "That seat is taken." You get to decide what thoughts enter your mind and which get escorted right back out. Boundaries don't mean you'll never hear shame again—they mean shame no longer has influence, attachment, or authority over your heart and mind.

Shame feeds on silence, agreement, and old patterns. Boundaries break that cycle. Saying "no" to shame shuts the door on its influence and creates space for truth, healing, and confidence to grow. Freedom is not passive; it's active, protective, intentional, and a form of spiritual warfare. The moment you refuse to give shame a voice, it loses power.

Establishing boundaries also means being aware of triggers—memories, conversations, comparisons, or mistakes—and refusing to let them dominate your thoughts. You don't have to control every circumstance, but you can control your response. Every boundary you set strengthens your identity in Christ and reinforces the truth that you are free.

When you practice boundaries consistently, shame loses its foothold. The same lies that once dominated your mind now pass like whispers in the wind. Each boundary you claim, each thought you reject, and each truth you declare reinforces a lifestyle of freedom that is sustainable and lasting.

### READ EPHESIANS 4:27 (KJV)

**Journal Prompt:**

How does shame try to slip back into your mind?

# Today's Challenge

Practice setting one boundary with shame today.
Say it out loud — even if you feel silly.
Your voice breaks shame's power.

# Day 3 – Rewriting Your Internal Narrative

Shame writes stories. If you aren't careful, those stories become your internal narrative, shaping how you think, feel, and act. Shame's narrative often sounds like: "I always mess things up," "I'm not good enough," "Something is wrong with me," "I should have known better," or "I don't deserve good things." These stories are not truths—they are lies you've agreed with, sometimes without realizing it.

Freedom rewrites your language because the words you speak inwardly become the life you live outwardly. Proverbs tells us, "Death and life are in the power of the tongue." This applies not only to what we say aloud but also to our internal dialogue. Your inner voice shapes your identity, your confidence, your expectations, and your emotional world. If shame narrates your life, it will feel small, heavy, unworthy, and uncertain. If truth narrates your life, it becomes grounded, hopeful, and healing.

Rewriting your narrative means intentionally choosing words that reflect God's perspective of you. Not: "I'm broken." But: "I'm being restored." Not: "I'm unworthy." But: "I'm deeply loved." Not: "I can't change." But: "God is transforming me." Not: "This is who I am." But: "This is who I was—not who I am becoming." Your words cultivate your emotional and spiritual atmosphere, inviting God's truth to define you instead of shame.

This process requires practice. You may stumble, repeat old narratives, or feel awkward. That's normal. Every time you choose truth over lie, however, you weaken shame's authority and strengthen God's voice in your life. Your internal language is your first defense against old patterns of guilt, insecurity, or self-condemnation.

The goal is a consistent alignment between your inner story and God's story for you. When your inner voice agrees with His, you carry confidence, hope, and freedom into every situation. Rewriting your narrative transforms your mind, shapes your heart, and rewires your identity. You are not what shame says; you are what God declares.

# Bible Reading

*READ JOEL 3:10 (KJV)*

**Journal Prompt:**

What internal statements do you repeat most often?

Write 5 statements today that rewrite your internal narrative.
Speak them out loud.
Write them again before bed.

This is where transformation becomes visible. Walking unashamed is not just about healing; it is about embodying the freedom God has already given you. A woman who walks unashamed is not perfect. She is grounded, secure, and aligned with truth. She knows her identity in Christ, refuses to shrink or hide, and carries herself with confidence rooted in God rather than in performance.

A woman who walks unashamed shows up fully, speaks boldly, loves freely, receives grace easily, apologizes without self-condemnation, forgives without spiraling, and makes mistakes without losing her sense of worth. She is not flawless—she is free. Walking unashamed does not mean insecurity, shame, or doubt will never appear. It means they no longer dictate your choices, define your identity, or control your life.

This woman has internalized the truth that God is her source. Her identity is no longer fragile, her worth is not negotiable, and her place in God's family is secure. She navigates relationships, work, and challenges from a position of freedom. She sets healthy boundaries, speaks truth, and lives authentically because she knows God's love, forgiveness, and restoration cover every imperfection.

Walking unashamed transforms not only your inner life but also how you engage with the world. Others see freedom, courage, and radiance. You become a reflection of God's restoration and a testimony to His power over shame. This lifestyle is a daily choice, an active posture of truth, a declaration that you belong wholly and completely to Him. When you walk unashamed, you are no longer shaped by shame's lies. You are defined by God's truth. You are free to live fully, love boldly, and embrace your calling. You are no longer hiding—you are thriving.

# Bible Reading

*READ PSALM 34:5 (KJV)*

**Journal Prompt:**
What does "walking unashamed" look like for you personally?

# Weekly Recap

This week, you learned to not just receive freedom but to live it. You practiced daily choices that reject shame, set boundaries to protect your mind, rewrote your internal narrative, and embraced the identity of a woman who walks unashamed.

You discovered that freedom is not passive—it is intentional, active, and sustained. You recognized that shame will always try to return, but it no longer has the authority it once held. By choosing truth, setting boundaries, and speaking life over yourself, you claimed a new normal: one where your identity, worth, and confidence come from God alone.

You are no longer the woman shame tried to shape you into. You are free from past patterns, unburdened by insecurity, and empowered to step into your purpose. Every thought you capture, every lie you reject, and every boundary you establish strengthens this new identity.

Shame may whisper, but your choices speak louder. Freedom is no longer occasional—it is habitual. It is no longer temporary—it is lifestyle. And it is yours to live daily.

# Weekly Prayer

Dear Father,

Thank you for leading me into a shame-free life.

Strengthen me to walk in freedom daily.

Help me choose truth over lies, boundaries over bondage, and identity over insecurity.

Let my life reflect Your healing, Your love, and Your grace.

In Jesus' name,
Amen.

Week Seven

Shame doesn't just attack your identity—it attacks your relationships. It whispers things like, "You're too much," "You're not enough," "They wouldn't love you if they knew the real you," and "You don't belong with people like them." Shame isolates because isolation is where it thrives. But God created you for connection—real, deep, meaningful connection. Not the surface-level kind where you smile and pretend everything's okay, but the kind where you can breathe, be honest, and be seen without fear.

Shame tells you to hide, to withdraw, to assume rejection. God calls you to the opposite: to heal, to draw near, to trust His acceptance, and to step into community. Healing does not happen in isolation; it happens in connection. God designed relationships as a place of comfort, accountability, encouragement, and transformation. Your past doesn't disqualify you. Your wounds don't make you a burden. Your healing does not need to be hidden.

God wants to restore your circle, not with just any people, but with those who can see you, hold you, walk with you without judgment, and call out the God in you—even on your hardest days. Belonging is not optional; it is essential. You are not meant to live isolated. You are created for connection, and God is leading you back to it.

When shame whispers that you're unworthy, remind yourself that God has already accepted you. Step into relationships with courage, knowing that healing multiplies when shared. Community is not just a support system—it is part of God's plan for your restoration.

# Bible Reading

**READ ECCLESIASTES 4:9 (KJV)**

**Journal Prompt:**

How has shame influenced your relationships?

Today's Challenge

Reach out to one person today you've unintentionally isolated yourself from.
A simple message is enough.

Shame teaches you to hide not only your past but also your heart. It encourages you to hold back, avoid vulnerability, stay guarded, pretend you're okay, and keep people at a distance. But connection requires courage—the courage to be honest, to be seen, and to say, "This is where I'm really at."

Being seen can feel scary. People cannot love the real version of you if they never meet her. The enemy knows this, which is why he whispers that vulnerability is dangerous. But when you choose to be seen by the right people, freedom grows. Vulnerability is holy because it opens the door for honesty, healing, and authentic connection.

Jesus modeled vulnerability. He shared openly with His disciples, wept in front of friends, asked for support, and allowed people to see Him fully. If Jesus lived vulnerably, you do not have to fear it. Often, the things you are afraid to say out loud are the very things that dismantle shame's power. Vulnerability does not weaken you; it strengthens your relationships and your identity in God.

Being seen is not about exposing every flaw to everyone; it is about choosing safe people, stepping into authenticity, and practicing honesty that aligns with God's truth. It is a step toward freedom and deeper connection. When you are willing to be seen, you invite God to multiply healing, encourage courage in others, and remind yourself that your identity is secure in Him, not in human approval.

# Bible Reading

## READ JAMES 5:16 (KJV)

**Journal Prompt:**

What do you fear people will think if they really knew you?

## Today's Challenge

Share one honest truth with someone safe today — even if it's small.

Healing requires the right relationships—not just any relationships. Some connections pull you back into shame, drain you, enable old patterns, reinforce lies, or make you feel "less than." God calls you to evaluate your circle and choose relationships that align with your healing.

Healthy relationships inspire you, challenge you, encourage you, speak truth, honor your growth, and support your journey. As God restores you, He also refines your circle. You may outgrow people—not because of rejection, but because of transformation. You will disconnect from certain voices, not out of harshness, but because healing creates boundaries where necessary.

You are allowed to prioritize relationships that strengthen your soul. You are allowed to walk away from connections that sabotage your freedom. God wants your circle to feel like oxygen—people who affirm, guide, and celebrate your healing, not just tolerate it. Choosing healthy relationships is not selfish; it is part of maintaining the life and freedom God has restored in you.

Scripture reminds us, "Bad company corrupts good character" (1 Corinthians 15:33). Wisdom is discerning which relationships support your freedom and which ones threaten it. God gives clarity, and He will guide you toward those who belong in your inner circle. Your choices in relationships affect your emotional, spiritual, and mental well-being.

Healthy relationships provide accountability, encouragement, and belonging. They reflect God's design for connection and serve as a tangible reminder that you are not alone. Step into these relationships with intentionality and confidence, knowing that God is orchestrating the right people into your life at the right time.

**READ 1 CORINTHIANS 15:33 (KJV)**

**Journal Prompt:**

Which relationships in your life strengthen you?

## Today's Challenge

Write a list of relationships that feel healthy, neutral, and unhealthy.
Pray for clarity on who belongs where.

One of shame's deepest wounds is the belief: "I don't belong." It shows up when you enter a room, join a group, walk into church, meet new people, or even draw near to God. Shame tells you that you are the outsider, the odd one out, the one people tolerate, not love, the one too broken or too different. But God has already spoken: "You belong."

Belonging is not based on perfection, performance, or past mistakes—it is inherited because you are God's. You belong in His presence, in healthy communities, in meaningful relationships, in places where your voice matters, and in rooms where healing and growth happen. You are part of God's household. You are family, not a guest or outsider.

Shame tries to disqualify you, but God's acceptance is permanent. When you know you belong, you stop shrinking, apologizing for existing, overthinking your worth, or worrying about being "too much" or "not enough." You show up fully, freely, and confidently. Belonging is not a feeling—it is a truth to stand in.

Entering relationships with this mindset changes your posture, choices, and interactions. You engage courageously, love intentionally, and walk without fear. God calls you to stand firmly in belonging, to embrace connection, and to cultivate community as a reflection of His love. This week, take steps into spaces and relationships with the declaration: "I belong here." Let it shape the way you participate, connect, and thrive.

# Bible Reading

### READ EPHESIANS 2:19 (KJV)

**Journal Prompt:**
When have you felt like you didn't belong?

Practice stepping into a space (physical or relational) with the mindset:
"I belong here."
Notice how it changes your posture.

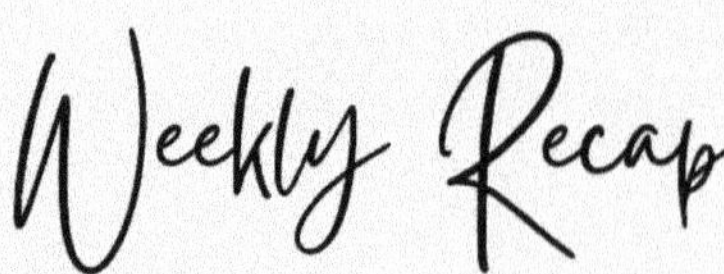

# Weekly Recap

This week, you broke shame's power in your relationships. You learned that shame isolates, but God restores. You discovered that courage is required to be seen, healthy relationships matter, and belonging is not earned—it is a truth to embrace.

Healing does not happen in hiding—it happens in community. God is restoring your circle, strengthening your connections, and guiding you into relationships that encourage freedom, honesty, and growth. You are learning to step into spaces with confidence, set boundaries where needed, and choose relationships that align with your healing.

You were never meant to walk alone. God surrounds you with the right people, at the right time, for the right purpose. Freedom in community is part of walking fully in your restored identity.

Dear Father,

Thank you for restoring connection in my life.

Thank You for healing the places shame isolated me.

Surround me with the right people, deepen my relationships, and help me walk confidently in true belonging.

Let community become a place of healing, strength, and joy.

In Jesus' name,
Amen.

Week Eight

# Day 1: A New Future Requires a New Identity

When shame ruled your life, it shaped your decisions, your relationships, your confidence, your expectations, and even your vision for the future. Every step you took was influenced by the lie that you were defined by past mistakes, flaws, or insecurities. But shame is no longer your identity, which means your future is no longer limited.

Your shame-free future begins with a new identity—one rooted in truth, not trauma; in grace, not guilt; in calling, not condemnation. God never asks shame who you are. He calls you by your real name: Daughter. Loved. Chosen. Whole. Worthy. Purposed. Set apart. Empowered. Your future does not flow from the lowest version of you—it flows from the rebuilt, restored, and Spirit-filled version.

Your next chapter is not determined by your past, your mistakes, your regrets, your insecurities, or your history. It is determined by God's Spirit working within you. You are not stepping into your old life with new confidence; you are stepping into a new life with a new identity. You are not called to live small, afraid, or ashamed. You are called to live spaciously, boldly, and Spirit-led.

This future is full of holy possibility. It invites you to move with courage, make decisions from freedom, and embrace opportunities without hesitation. Your shame-free life is not about perfection—it is about walking faithfully into the path God has prepared.

Because your identity is secure in Him, your future is no longer fragile or uncertain. You are stepping forward as a woman who is healed, chosen, empowered, and deeply loved. Every fear, every doubt, and every lingering tie to shame is being replaced by confidence, purpose, and God-given authority.

Your new identity is the lens through which you now view life. Decisions, relationships, and opportunities flow from who God says you are. You are not defined by the past; you are defined by Him. Your steps are guided by His Spirit, your voice speaks truth, and your life reflects freedom. This is the foundation of a future that shame cannot touch, diminish, or claim.

**READ REVELATION 21:5 (KJV)**

**Journal Prompt:**

How has shame shaped your expectations for the future?

Today's Challenge

Write one sentence describing the future you want to walk into — as if shame
never existed.

Shame doesn't just attack who you are—it attacks what you're called to do. It whispers lies like, "You're not ready," "You're not spiritual enough," "You'll mess it up," "Someone else could do it better," or "God can't use someone like you." But God never calls perfect people. He calls willing ones.

Throughout Scripture, God chose imperfect people to accomplish extraordinary purposes. Moses doubted himself, Jeremiah felt too young, Gideon felt unqualified, Peter felt too sinful, David felt flawed, Paul felt guilty. Shame tried to silence them, but God spoke louder. Your calling is always bigger than your insecurity, your past, or your wounds.

Stepping into your purpose is terrifying to shame. Purpose makes you a threat to darkness. It positions you to heal, help, lead, and influence others. Your purpose is not something you earn—it is God-embedded. The world needs your voice, your story, your gifts, and your testimony. God's plan for you is unique and strategic, and shame cannot disqualify what He has already prepared.

Your calling is alive and active, waiting for you to step boldly. Courage is required, but God equips you for every assignment. Moving in obedience, even when you feel unready, is how freedom grows. God will provide the wisdom, tools, and strength for the journey.

You are empowered to walk into your calling with confidence. Fear does not define you. Shame does not dictate your limits. God's purposes are bigger than your doubts. When you step forward in faith, you participate in His story of redemption—not just for yourself, but for others who will be impacted by your obedience and courage.

# Bible Reading

**Journal Prompt:**

What purpose have you been avoiding because of shame?

Write down one calling God has whispered to you — even if it scares you.
Sit with it.
Pray over it.
Let God reignite it.

Shame shrinks your life. It limits your dreams, your voice, your confidence, and even your world. It convinces you to stay small, safe, and unseen. But freedom expands your life. God invites you to a larger life—a life shame told you was off-limits.

A shame-free life means taking up space, speaking with confidence, pursuing dreams you shelved, saying yes to God-sized opportunities, stepping into leadership, and boldly entering rooms you once felt unqualified for. Expansion does not require fearlessness. Courage is not the absence of fear—it is choosing truth over fear and obedience over limitation.

You are a woman of calling, and called women live expansively. The Holy Spirit stretches you, not to overwhelm, but to grow you into the life He designed. This is not stepping backward—it is stepping forward, bigger, and deeper. God asks you to embrace life courageously, to occupy space intentionally, and to trust Him in the process.

Expansion is spiritual, emotional, relational, and practical. It includes confidence in relationships, generosity in influence, boldness in opportunities, and resilience in challenges. God's invitation is clear: "Enlarge the place of your tent... do not hold back; lengthen your cords, strengthen your stakes" (Isaiah 54:2). You do not expand by your own strength; you expand because God is with you.

Your life is designed to grow in every dimension. Fear of failure or past shame cannot contain you. God's purposes for your life are wide, deep, and abundant. You are stepping into freedom, authority, and purpose that reflect His kingdom. Each bold step is a declaration that shame no longer limits your potential.

# Bible Reading

## READ ISAIAH 54:2 (KJV)

**Journal Prompt:**

What part of your life feels too small?

Do one thing today that symbolizes expansion — something small but bold.

# Day 4 - Your Future Is Shame-Free, Live Like It

God didn't deliver you from shame to survive; He delivered you to live fully. A shame-free life is peaceful, confident, connected, purpose-driven, spiritually anchored, emotionally healthy, identity-secure, and obedient.

Living without shame does not mean life is easy. It means facing life differently: from truth, strength, and wholeness. Decisions are made without fear, relationships chosen without insecurity, and opportunities pursued without self-doubt. You respond to challenges with resilience and show up to your life with confidence.

Your future is free—not because of your effort, but because God has completed the work. Shame was a chapter, not your story. You are stepping into a life where shame has no authority, no voice, no influence, and no control. You are healed, restored, redeemed, strengthened, anointed, called, confident, and enough.

Your future is not fragile. It is secure because your identity in Christ is secure. Freedom is not symbolic; it is a spiritual reality. You are free in God's eyes. How you live each day is a reflection of that freedom. Walk boldly, make decisions courageously, pursue dreams fully, and speak truth over your life. Your story is no longer defined by shame—it is defined by God's power, grace, and love.

# Bible Reading

**READ JOHN 8:36 (KJV)**

Journal Prompt:
What does a shame-free future look like for you?

Write a declaration describing your shame-free future.
Read it out loud as a prophetic statement.

# Weekly Recap

This week, you stepped into the future God prepared for you—a future shame cannot touch. You learned that a new identity creates a new future, shame cannot silence your calling, your life is meant to expand, and your future is secure and shame-free.

You are not the woman who began this study. You are stronger, clearer, healthier, more grounded, more confident, and more free. Shame no longer defines you, your past no longer controls you, and your wounds no longer disqualify you.

Your new beginning is alive, Spirit-led, and full of possibility. You are walking forward as a woman healed, restored, and empowered. Your identity shapes your choices, your courage drives your steps, and your faith opens doors to the life God has designed. This is your new chapter—a life free from shame and full of purpose.

# Weekly Prayer

Dear Father,

Thank You for this journey from shame to freedom.

Thank You for healing my heart, restoring my identity, and revealing my purpose.

Help me live boldly, faithfully, and confidently in the future You've prepared for me.

Let this truth anchor me every day: I am free.

In Jesus' name,
Amen.

Sweet Sister,

If you've made it this far, I want you to know how proud I am of you. This study wasn't easy. You faced painful memories, confronted old lies, revisited places shame once tried to bury, and chose truth every single day.

That is courage.  That is healing.  That is the work of the Holy Spirit within you.  You are not the same woman who began this journey. You are stronger, softer, bolder, and more aligned with God's heart for you. You have stepped out of the shadows of shame built— and into the light God created you to live in.

My prayer is that you won't stop here.  Continue choosing truth.  Continue choosing freedom.  Continue choosing connection.  Continue choosing courage.  Continue choosing yourself.  And every time shame tries to whisper again—and it will—remember this: You do not belong to shame. **You belong to God.**

Walk boldly into the future He designed for you. Walk confidently into the call He placed on your life. Walk freely into the identity He restored.  You are loved. You are chosen. You are enough. You are whole. You are free. And you are His.

If this study stirred something in you... If you're craving connection... If you're ready to build real relationships... I want to personally invite you into two communities built exactly for that:

**Mission Driven Sisters:** A global sisterhood for women who want authentic friendship, support, growth, and faith-filled conversations. Meet me there at MissionDrivenSisters.com

**Mission Driven Church:** An online church without walls — small groups, prayer, teaching, and a family that actually walks life with you. Visit MissionDrivenChurch.com to do life and change the world with us.

You don't have to pretend.  You don't have to isolate yourself to feel safe.  You don't have to be strong alone. There is a place for you — a real one. And it's waiting.

I am so proud of you.

All my love,

Bridget

# Continue Your Journey Toward Freedom

What you've just worked through is only one part of a bigger story.

The *You Are Not Called* series was created to help Christian women break free from the emotional struggles that quietly keep them stuck—often beneath the surface of faith, responsibility, and strength.

Each book in the series focuses on a different area where many women feel trapped, overwhelmed, or disconnected, including anger, anxiety, loneliness, fear, and shame.

While each study can be read on its own, the greatest transformation often happens when these truths are layered together over time.

If this book resonated with you, you're not alone—and you don't have to stop here.

## The *You Are Not Called* Series
Continue your journey with the other studies in the series:

### You Are Not Called to Be Angry
*A Bible Study for Christian Women Ready to Break Free from Anger*

### You Are Not Called to Be Anxious
*A Bible Study for Christian Women Ready to Break Free from Anxiety*

### You Are Not Called to Be Alone
*A Bible Study for Christian Women Ready to Break Free from Loneliness*

### You Are Not Called to Be Afraid
*A Bible Study for Christian Women Ready to Break Free from Fear*

### You Are Not Called to Be Ashamed
*A Bible Study for Christian Women Ready to Break Free from Shame*

Each book builds on the biblical truth about who you are and your calling — helping you heal deeply, renew your mind, and walk forward in the freedom God has always intended for you.

## A Final Word Before You Go

You don't have to rush this process. Healing is not a race—it's a relationship.

As you continue through the series, allow God to meet you where you are, speak truth into the places that feel tender, and gently lead you forward. You are not behind. You are not broken. And you are not alone on this journey.

God has more for you—and freedom is closer than you think.

# Free Resources

Hey there, superstar!

   You've made it through the book, and I'm so proud of you. But let's be real - reading is just the first step. Now it's time to put all this good stuff into practice. And because I'm not about to send you out there empty-handed, I've got some awesome resources to help you on your journey.

   Think of these as your anger management toolkit. They're like the Swiss Army knife of emotional growth - versatile, handy, and they might just save you in a pinch (though maybe don't try to use them to open a can or cut down a small tree).

To access the resources, simply create your free account at www.youarenotcalled.com.

Inside, you'll have to the above resources plus much more!